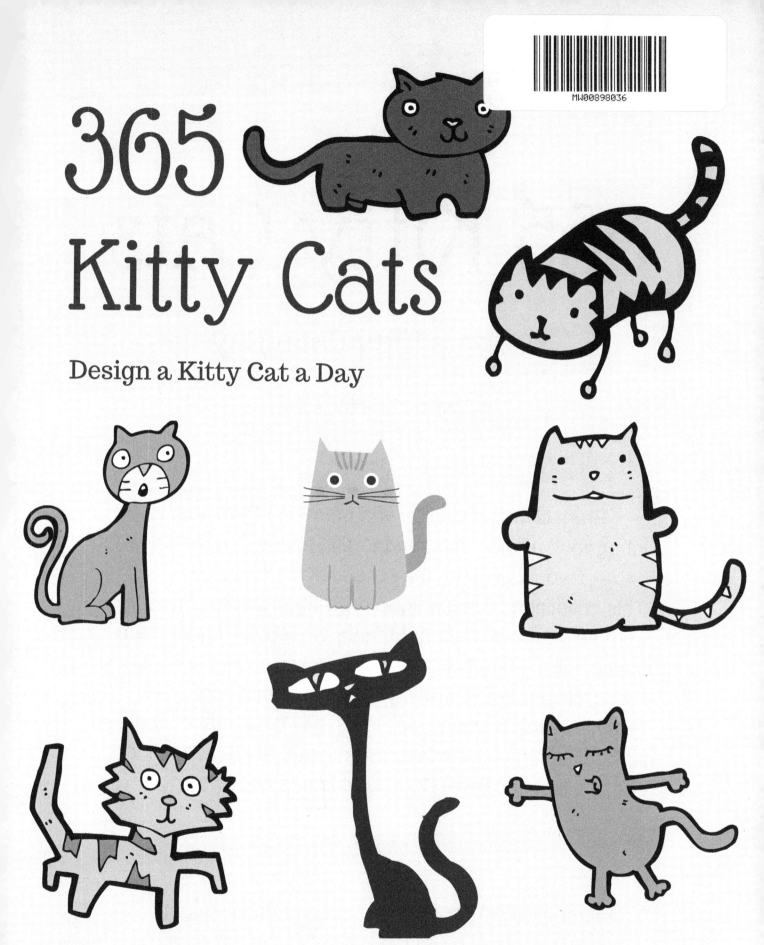

365 Kitty Cats

Design a Kitty Cat a Day

by Lisa & Madeline Larson

365 Kitty Cats

Design a Kitty Cat a Day

by Lisa & Madeline Larson

From climbing calicos and pouncing Persians, to outrageous orange cats, and terrific tuxies~ no matter what you call them, they are all KITTY CATS!
This collection of 365 unique drawing prompts allows you create your own cattery of fantastic felines. Make them simple, silly, or sophisticated~ whatever strikes your fancy.
If you like to draw, you will love this book.
Terrific for artists of any skill level, this book makes a great gift for Christmas, birthdays, Hanukkah, home schooling, or just because. Don't let this one get away!

available on CreateSpace.com and Amazon.com

My happy kitty cat

My spiky kitty cat

My golden kitty cat

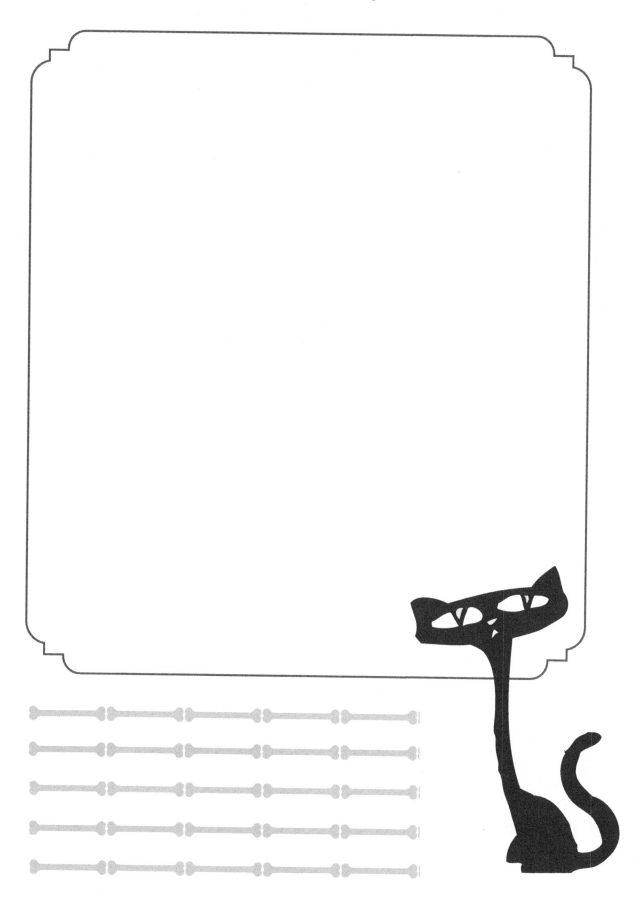

My cookie kitty cat

My goofy kitty cat

My little kitty cat

My toothy kitty cat

My hairless kitty cat

My baby kitty cat

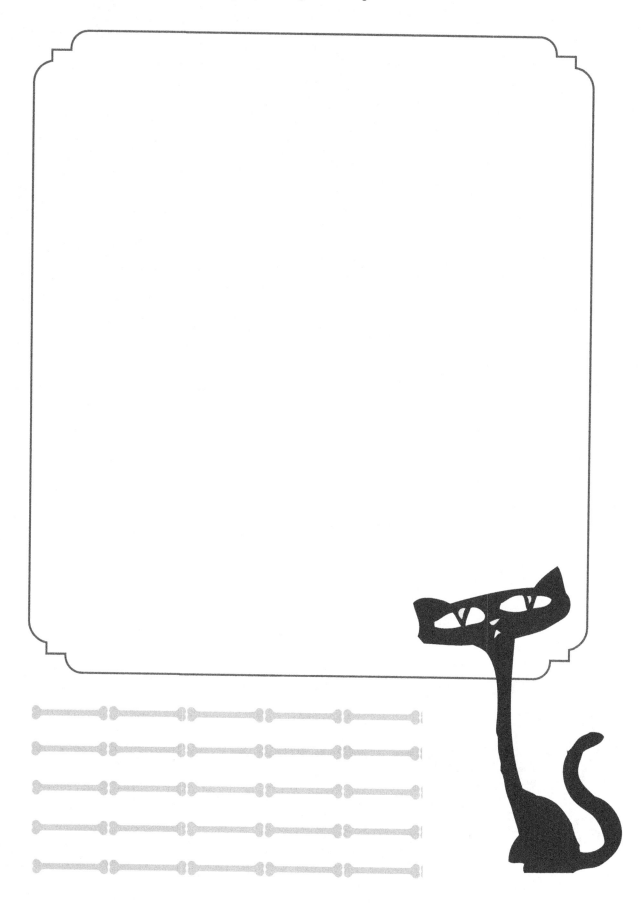

My pretty kitty cat

My pink kitty cat

My cowboy kitty cat

My pumpkin kitty cat

My freaky kitty cat

My panda kitty cat

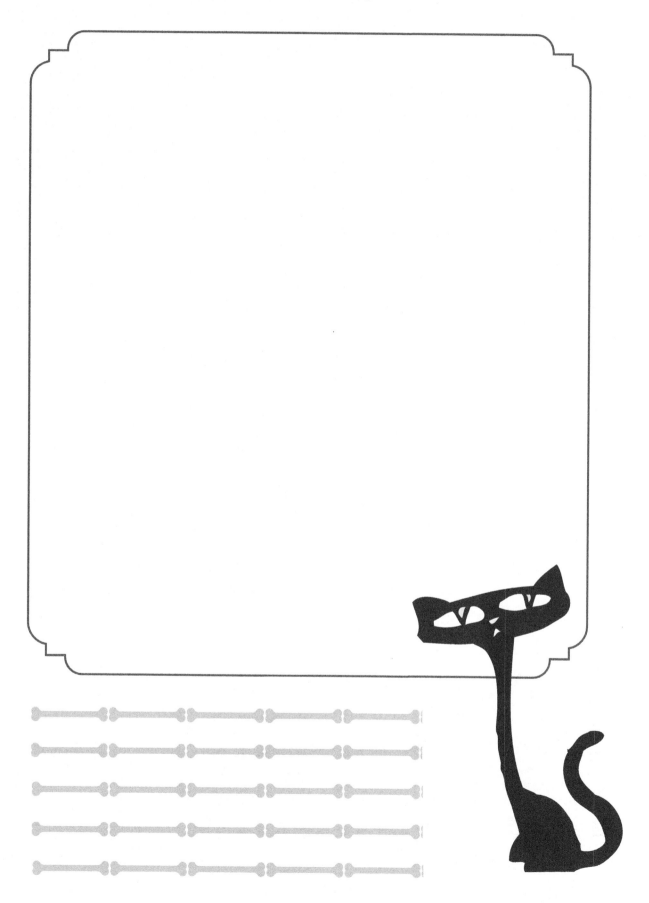

My tiara kitty cat

My long clawed kitty cat

My summer kitty cat

My wiggly kitty cat

My rainy kitty cat

My long eye-lashed kitty cat

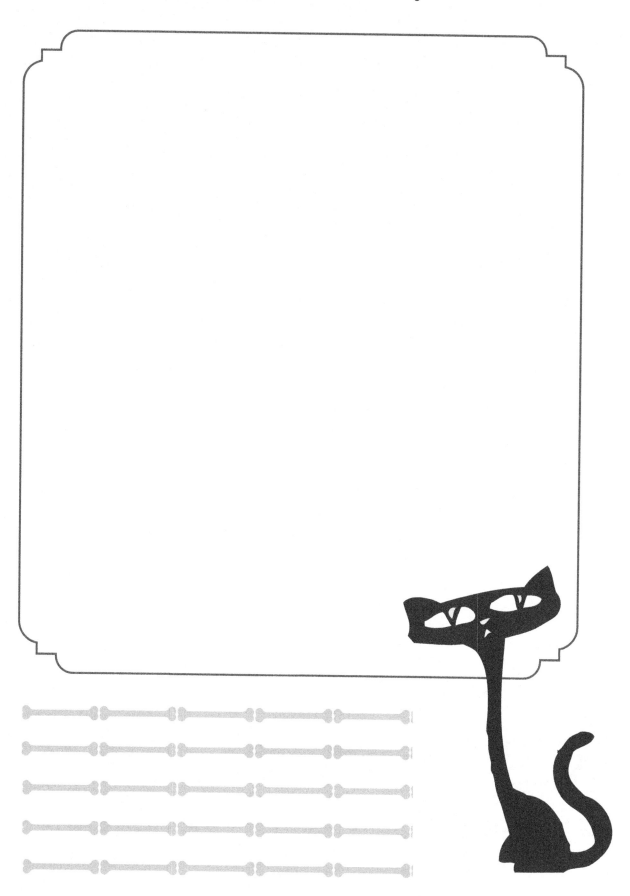

My violet kitty cat

My Hawaiian kitty cat

My tuxedo kitty cat

My strawberry kitty cat

My emerald kitty cat

My singing kitty cat

My happy kitty cat

My frozen kitty cat

My cherry kitty cat

My sad kitty cat

My blue-eyed kitty cat

My speedy kitty cat

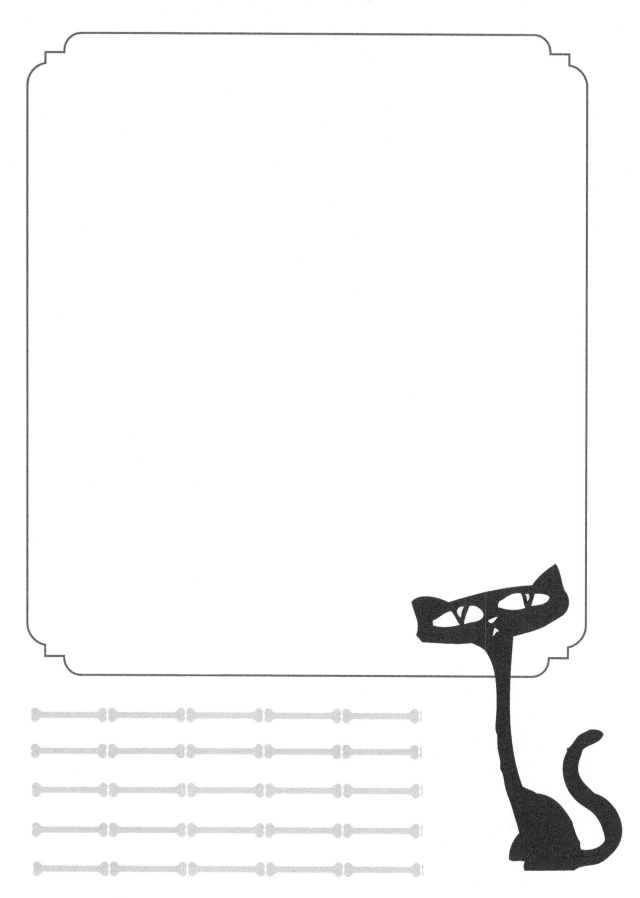

My gingerbread kitty cat

My copper kitty cat

My owl kitty cat

My mommy kitty cat

My ice cream kitty cat

My lavender kitty cat

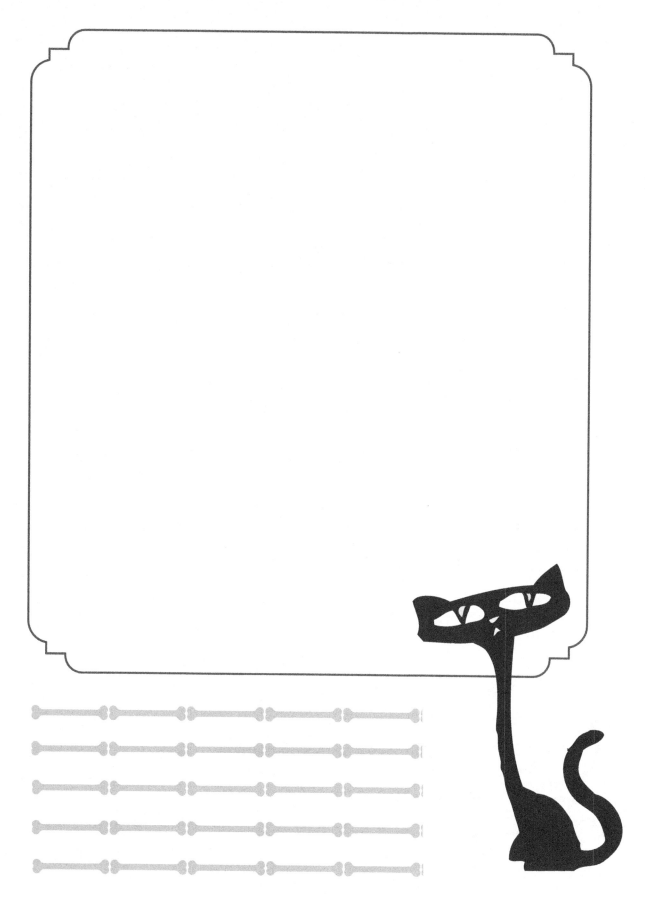

My intelligent kitty cat

My police officer kitty cat

My grinning kitty cat

My bumblebee kitty cat

My masked kitty cat

My soccer kitty cat

My green spotted kitty cat

My seahorse kitty cat

My lipstick kitty cat

My giant kitty cat

My chili pepper kitty cat

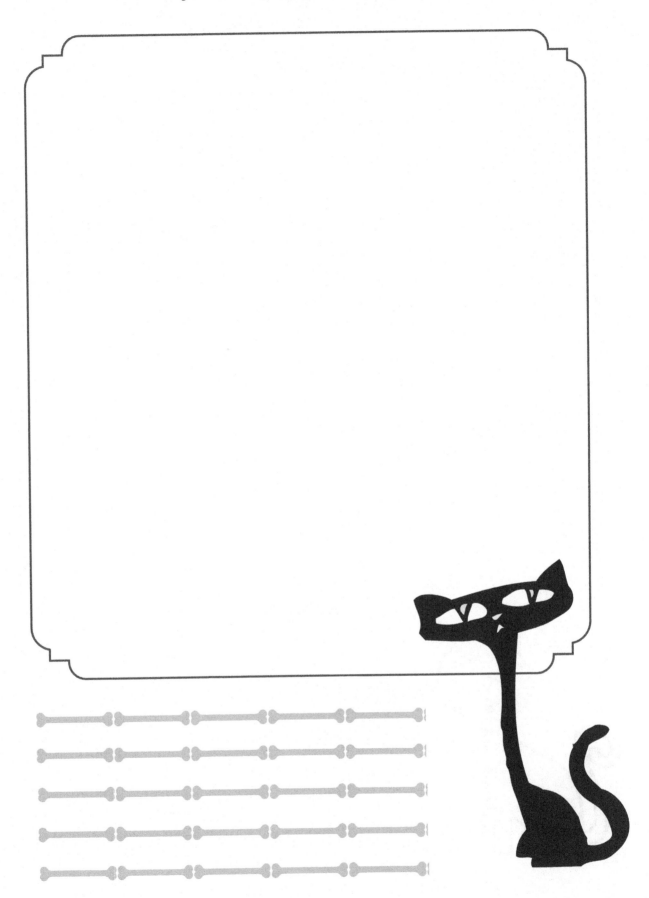

My quiet kitty cat

My money kitty cat

My birthday kitty cat

My hairless kitty cat

My cotton candy kitty cat

My water kitty cat

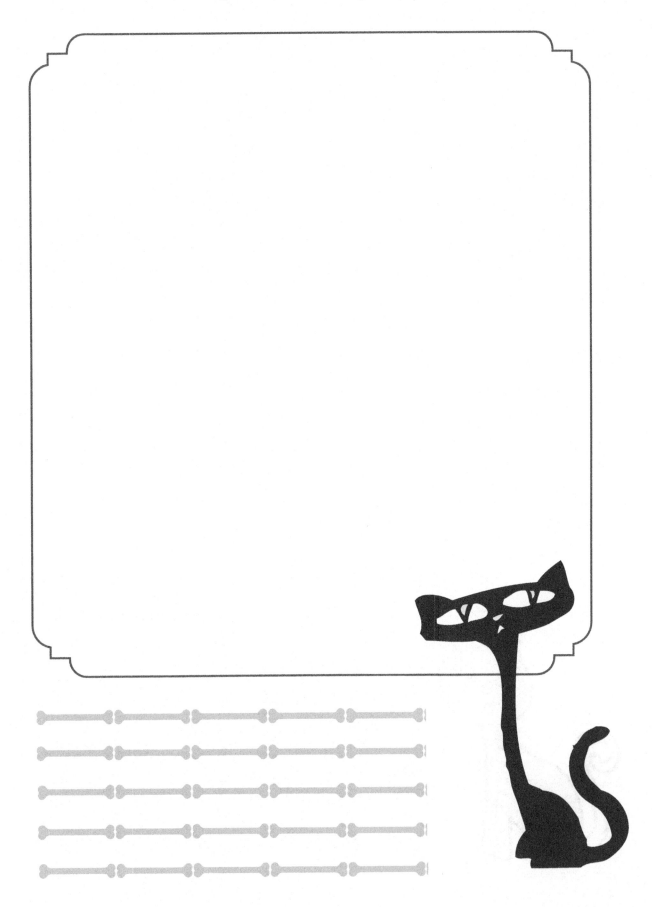

My yellow striped kitty cat

My happy kitty cat

My apple kitty cat

My friendly kitty cat

My prickly kitty cat

My silvery kitty cat

My pageant kitty cat

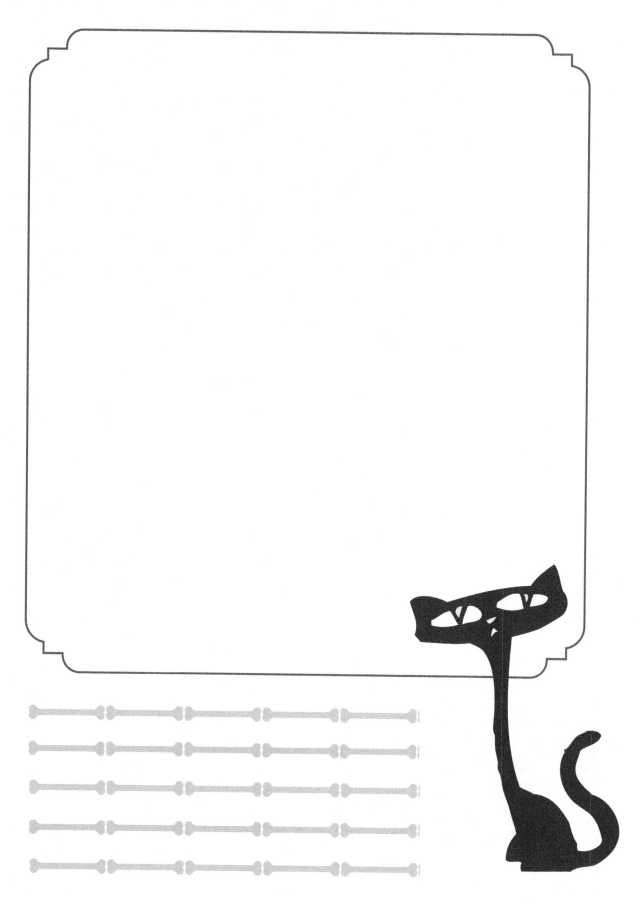

My ravenous kitty cat

My frosty kitty cat

My angel kitty cat

My red spotted kitty cat

My old kitty cat

My chubby kitty cat

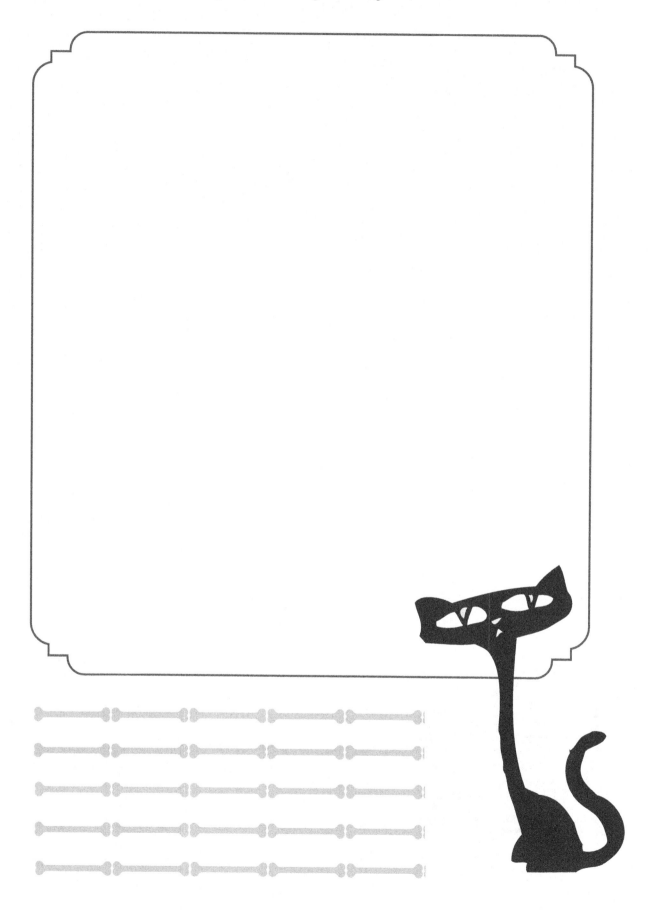

My white kitty cat

My hat wearing kitty cat

My elf kitty cat

My screeching kitty cat

My tiger kitty cat

My royal kitty cat

My 2 clawed spotted kitty cat

My autumn kitty cat

My sapphire kitty cat

My windy kitty cat

My shark kitty cat

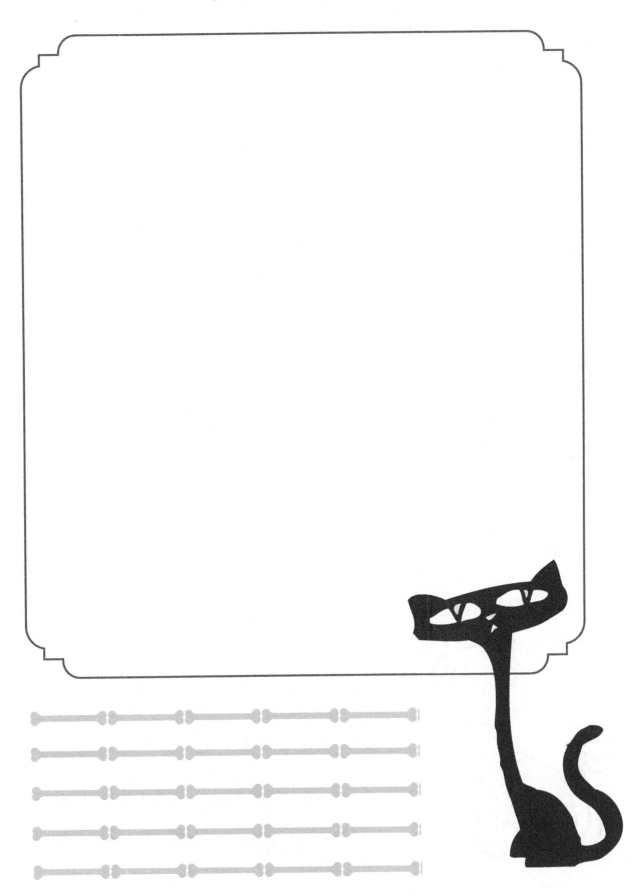

My donut kitty cat

My aqua kitty cat

My actor kitty cat

My brown eyed kitty cat

My berserk kitty cat

My musical kitty cat

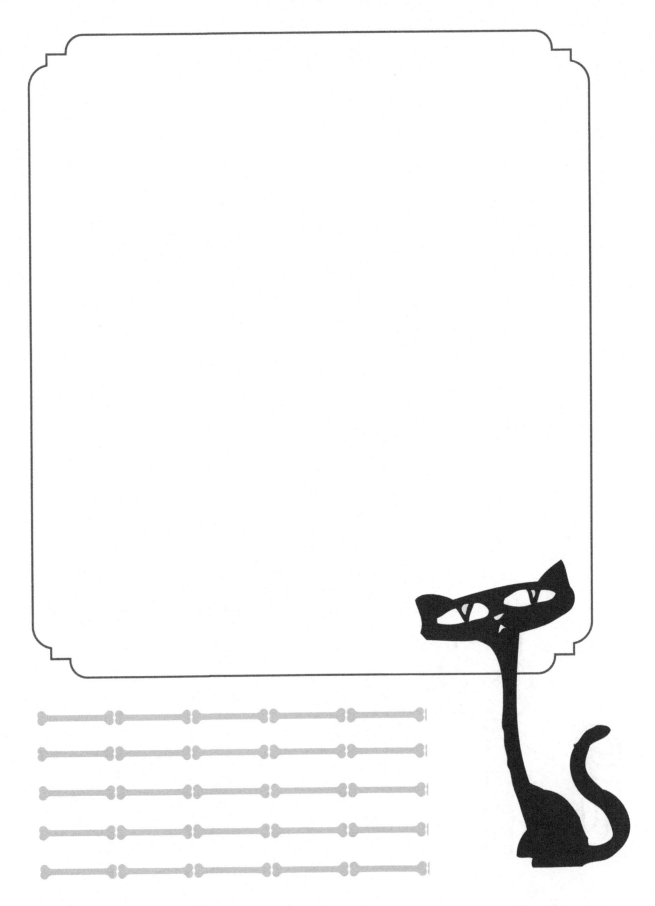

My fancy kitty cat

My happy kitty cat

My orange eyed kitty cat

My lantern kitty cat

My Swiss cheese kitty cat

My towering kitty cat

My bearded kitty cat

My brother kitty cat

My cupcake kitty cat

My daisy kitty cat

My moon kitty cat

My fire truck kitty cat

My lemonade kitty cat

My spider kitty cat

My sneezing kitty cat

My baseball kitty cat

My blue spotted kitty cat

My duck billed kitty cat

My tiny kitty cat

My quilted kitty cat

My muscular kitty cat

My popcorn kitty cat

My cute kitty cat

My Picasso kitty cat

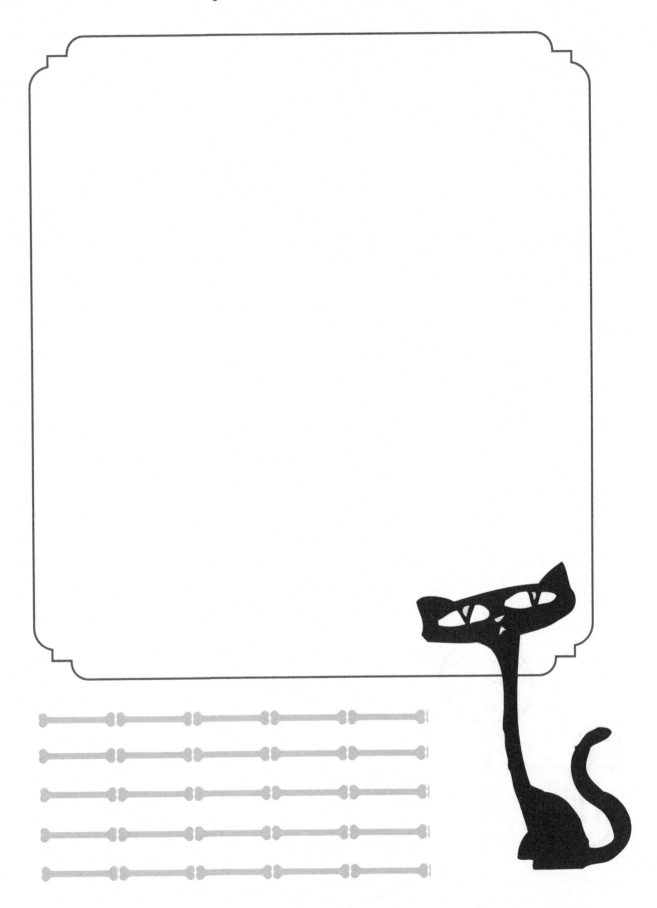

My fairy kitty cat

My electric kitty cat

My swimming kitty cat

My green striped kitty cat

My puffy kitty cat

My purring kitty cat

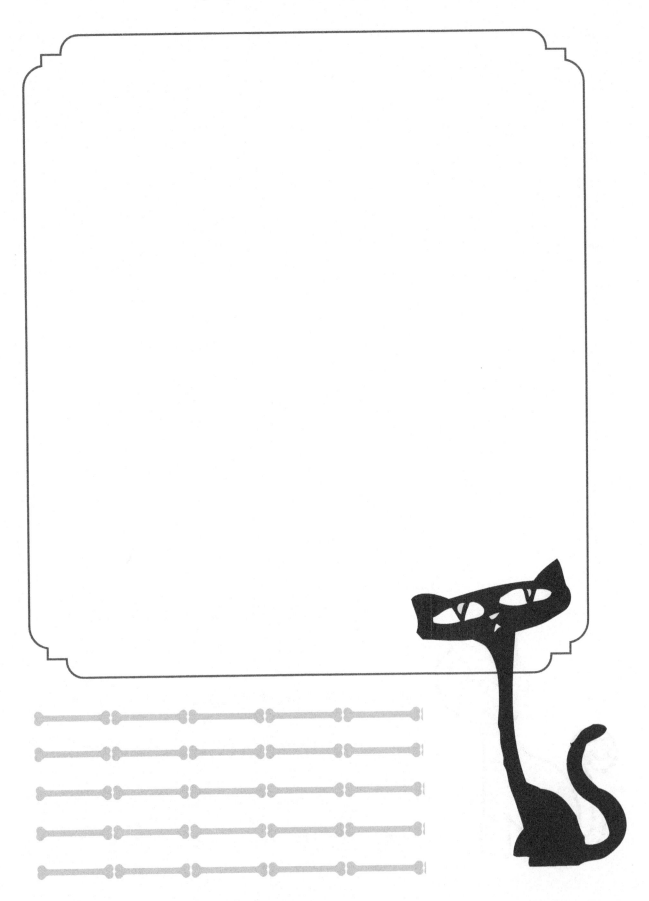

My tap dancing kitty cat

My happy kitty cat

My jellyfish kitty cat

My polka dot kitty cat

My charming kitty cat

My banana kitty cat

My black spotted kitty cat

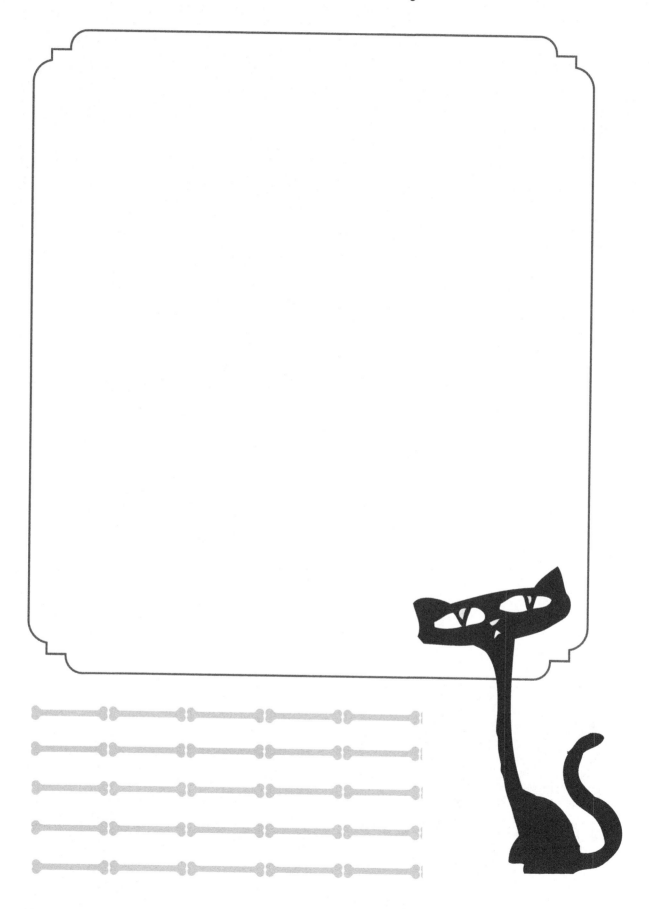

My crooked kitty cat

My skinny kitty cat

My gray kitty cat

My scarf wearing kitty cat

My bat winged kitty cat

My scary kitty cat

My zebra kitty cat

My queen kitty cat

My long tailed kitty cat

My winter kitty cat

My villainous kitty cat

My daffodil kitty cat

My chocolate kitty cat

My broom kitty cat

My witchy kitty cat

My sugarplum kitty cat

My braided kitty cat

My beefy kitty cat

My ruby kitty cat

My fiery kitty cat

My ballerina kitty cat

My t-rex kitty cat

My majestic kitty cat

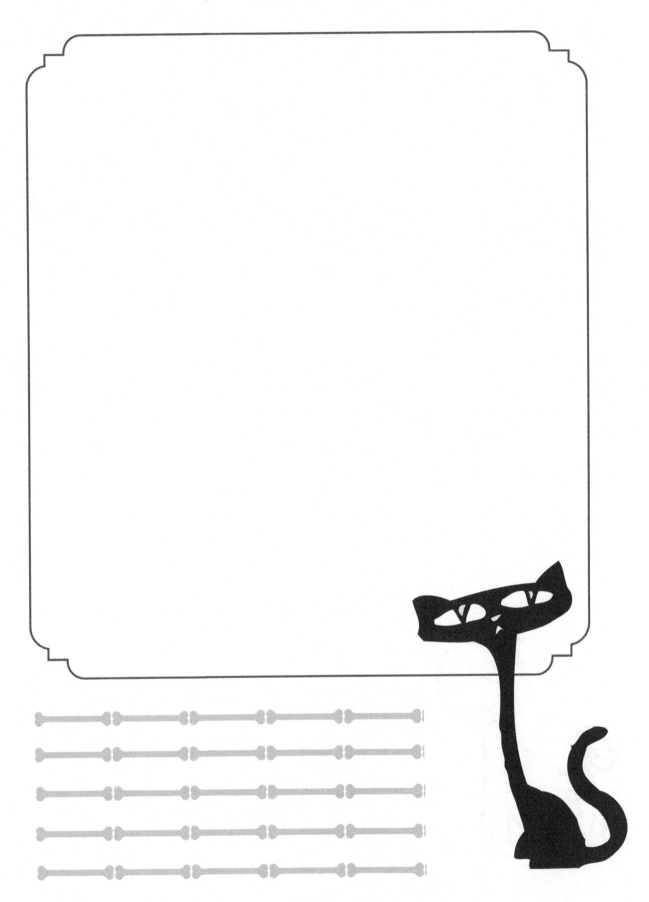

My monkey kitty cat

My happy kitty cat

My wet kitty cat

My pancake kitty cat

My naughty kitty cat

My whiskered kitty cat

My grandpa kitty cat

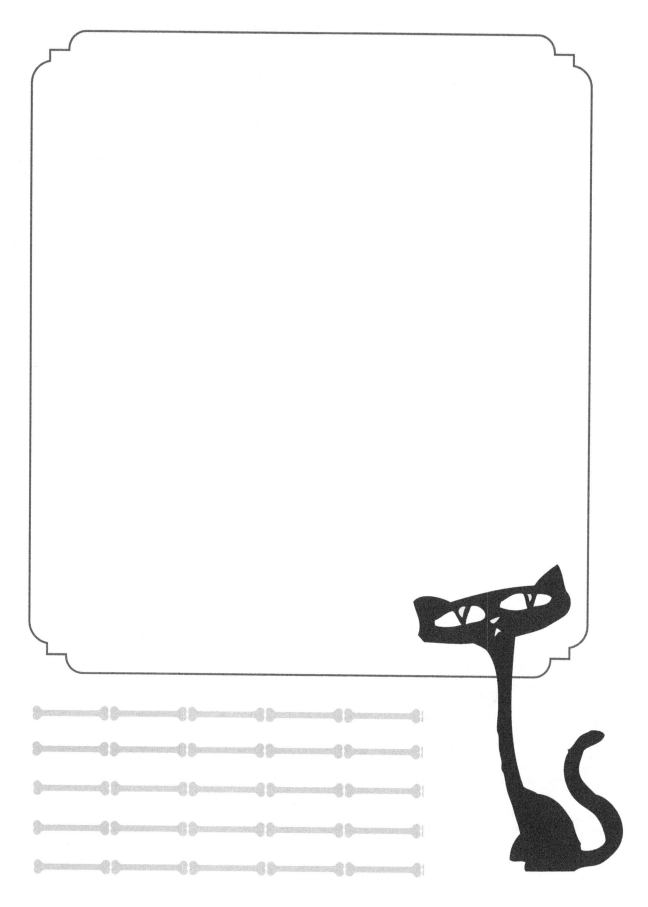

My cinnamon roll kitty cat

My iris kitty cat

My martian kitty cat

My teacher kitty cat

My macaroni kitty cat

My flying kitty cat

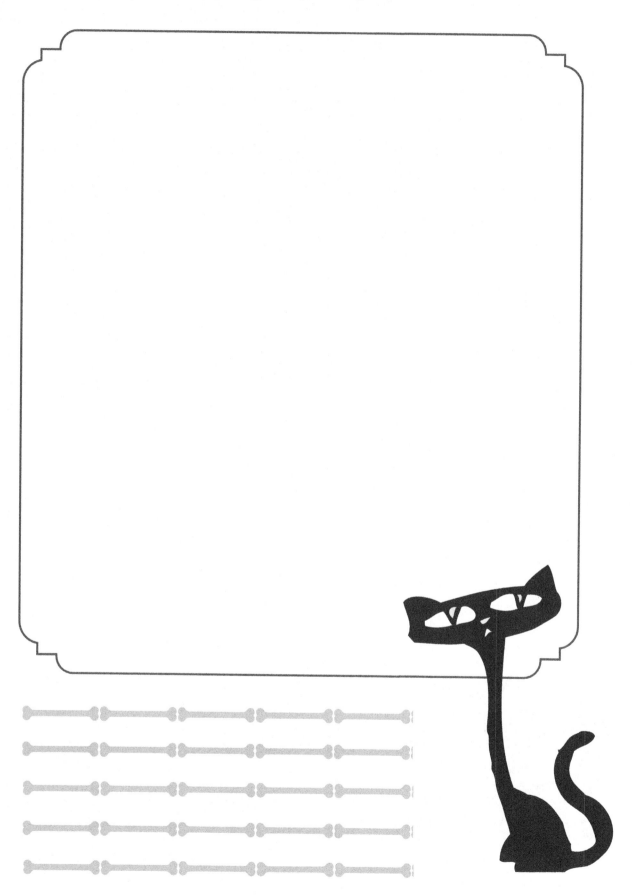

My snake kitty cat

My tennis kitty cat

My pink spotted kitty cat

My garden kitty cat

My sushi kitty cat

My tall kitty cat

My mummy kitty cat

My chameleon kitty cat

My precious kitty cat

My horn blowing kitty cat

My strong kitty cat

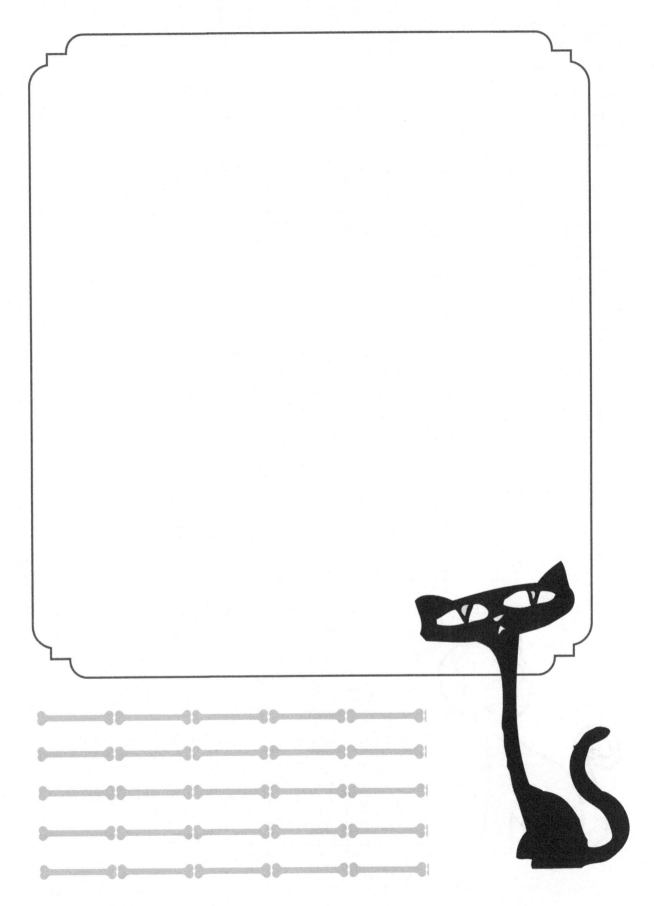

My seaweed kitty cat

My freckled kitty cat

My blue striped kitty cat

My lollipop kitty cat

My arching kitty cat

My bicycling kitty cat

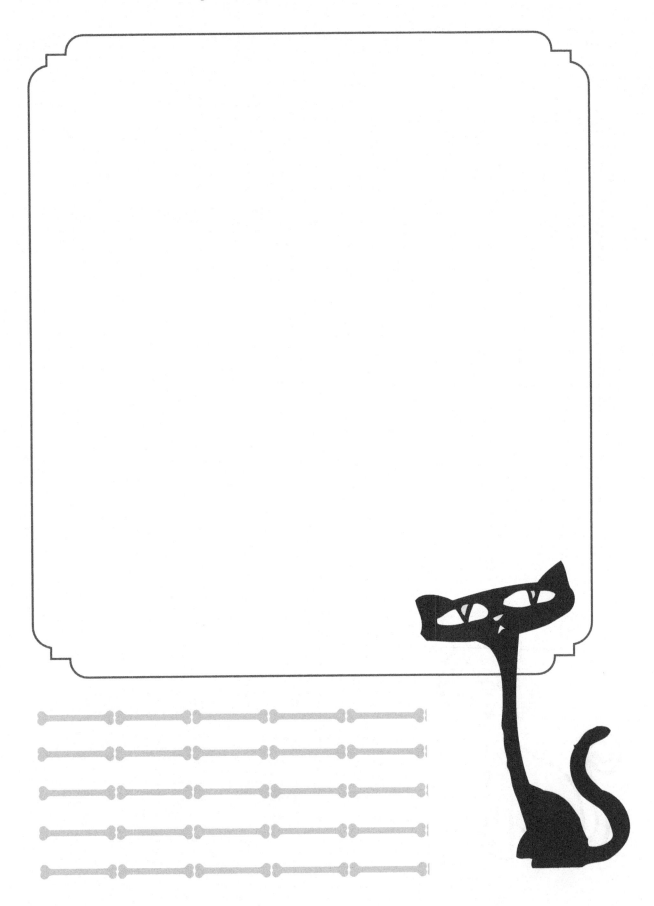

My metal kitty cat

My deep sea kitty cat

My princess kitty cat

My wedding kitty cat

My afraid kitty cat

My brown spotted kitty cat

My long kitty cat

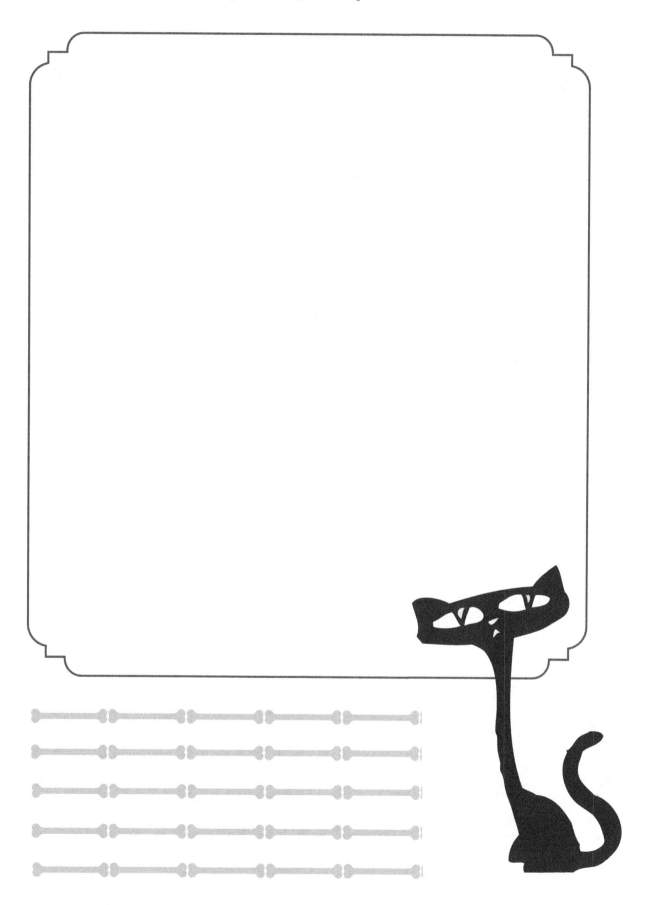

My twin kitty cat

My blue kitty cat

My glasses wearing kitty cat

My dragon winged kitty cat

My giraffe kitty cat

My playful kitty cat

My stub tailed kitty cat

My spring kitty cat

My water colored kitty cat

My coconut kitty cat

My top hat kitty cat

My feasting kitty cat

My caterpillar kitty cat

My floating kitty cat

My taco kitty cat

My dragonfly kitty cat

My diamond kitty cat

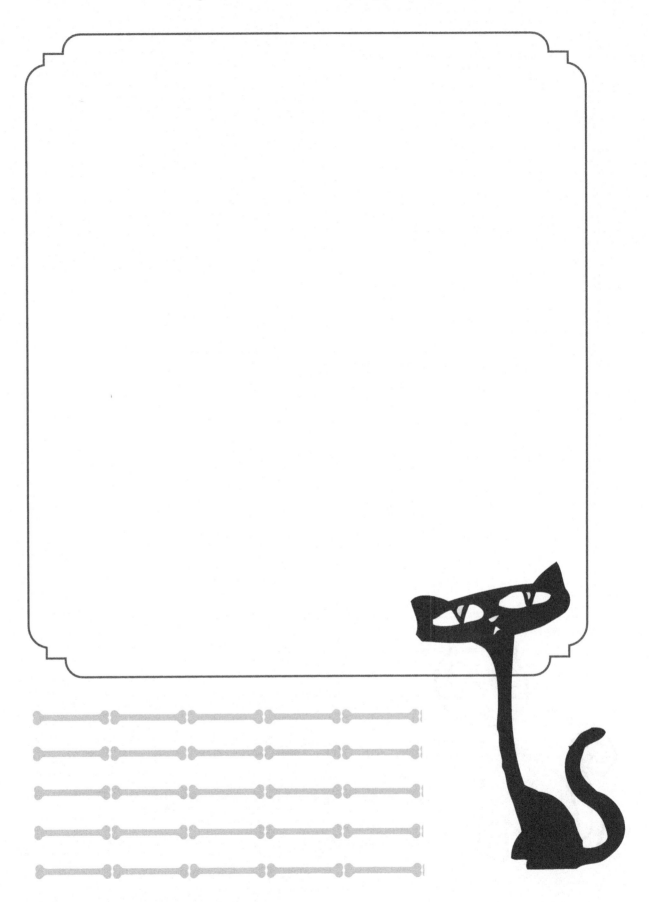

My snowman kitty cat

My banshee kitty cat

My skateboard kitty cat

My coffee kitty cat

My beach kitty cat

My green eyed kitty cat

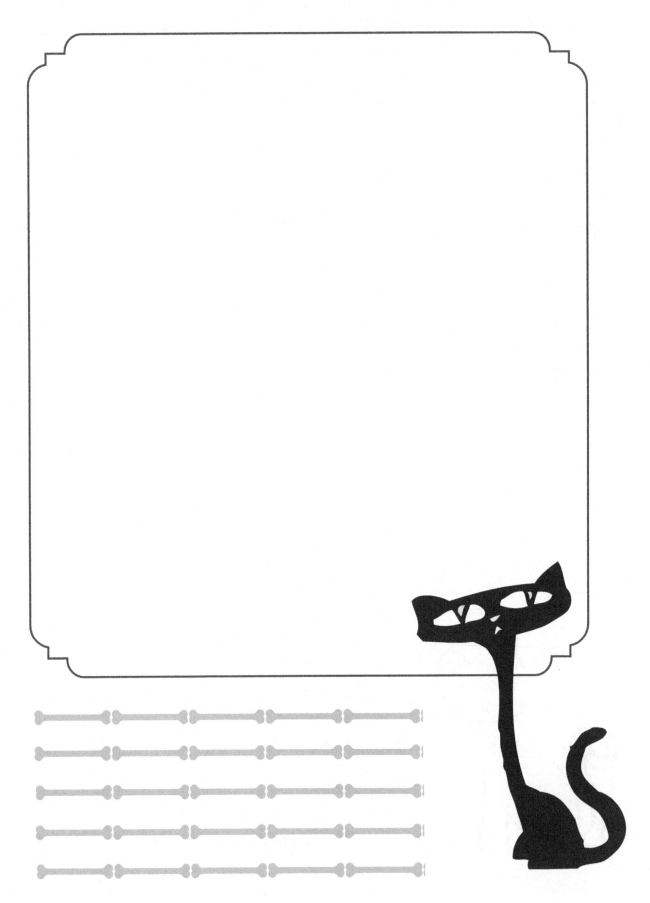

My french fry kitty cat

My wooden kitty cat

My balloon kitty cat

My mustached kitty cat

My daddy kitty cat

My sundae kitty cat

My holly berry kitty cat

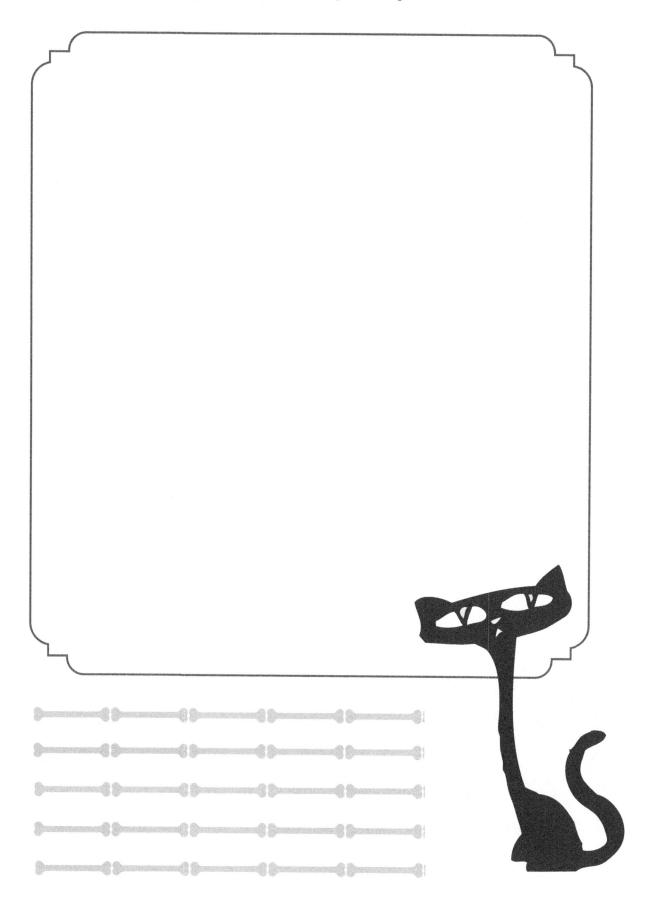

My sunshine kitty cat

My soldier kitty cat

My watermelon kitty cat

My ladybug kitty cat

My pickle kitty cat

My football kitty cat

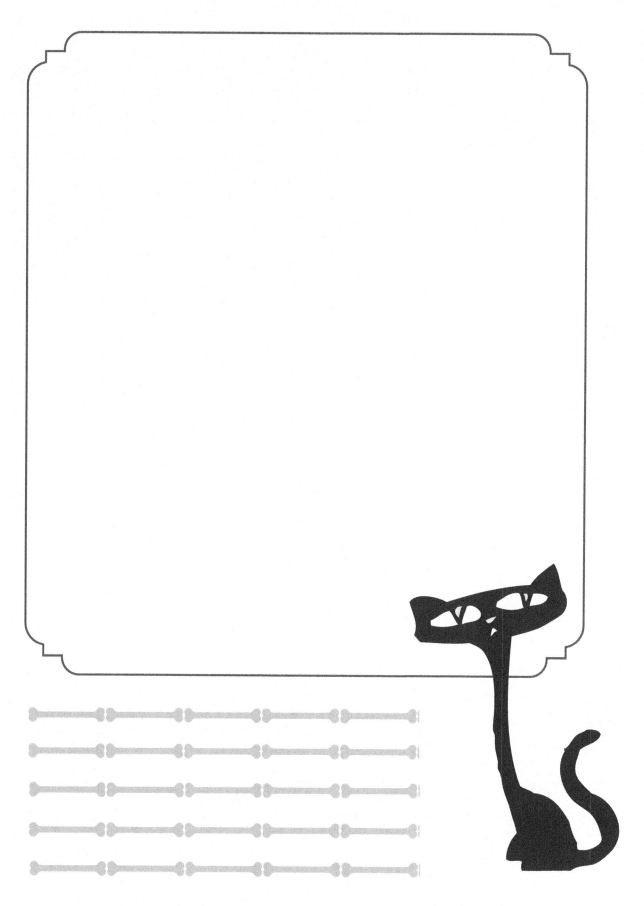

My orange spotted kitty cat

My octopus kitty cat

My rotten kitty cat

My short kitty cat

My delicate kitty cat

My sunflower kitty cat

My bow tie wearing kitty cat

My antlered kitty cat

My alien kitty cat

My froggy kitty cat

My ninja kitty cat

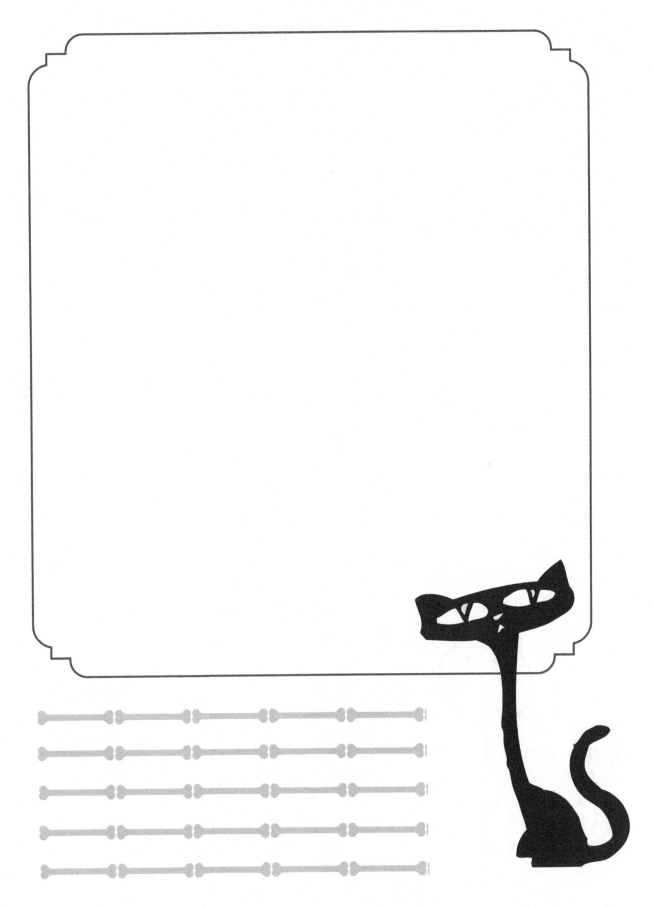

My pink striped kitty cat

My veiled kitty cat

My frightened kitty cat

My scratching kitty cat

My balancing kitty cat

My platinum kitty cat

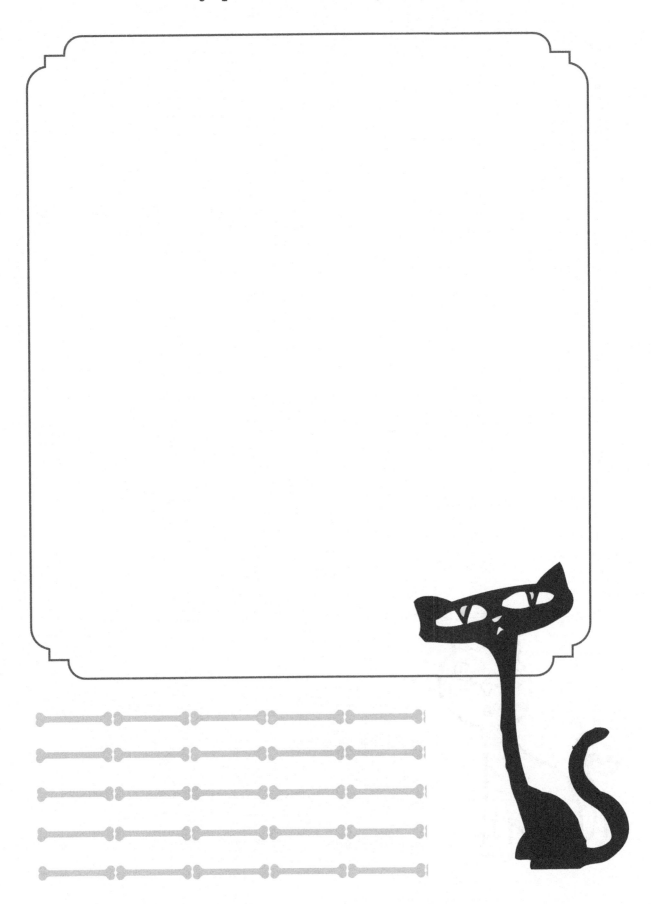

My starfish kitty cat

My wooden kitty cat

My candy kitty cat

My tusked kitty cat

My white spotted kitty cat

My dwarf kitty cat

My fuzzy kitty cat

My green kitty cat

My silly kitty cat

My butterfly winged kitty cat

My monstrous kitty cat

My elephant kitty cat

My king kitty cat

My ring tailed kitty cat

My angry kitty cat

My stained glass kitty cat

My leafy kitty cat

My race car kitty cat

My waffle kitty cat

My star kitty cat

My peachy kitty cat

My weird kitty cat

My upside down kitty cat

My butterscotch kitty cat

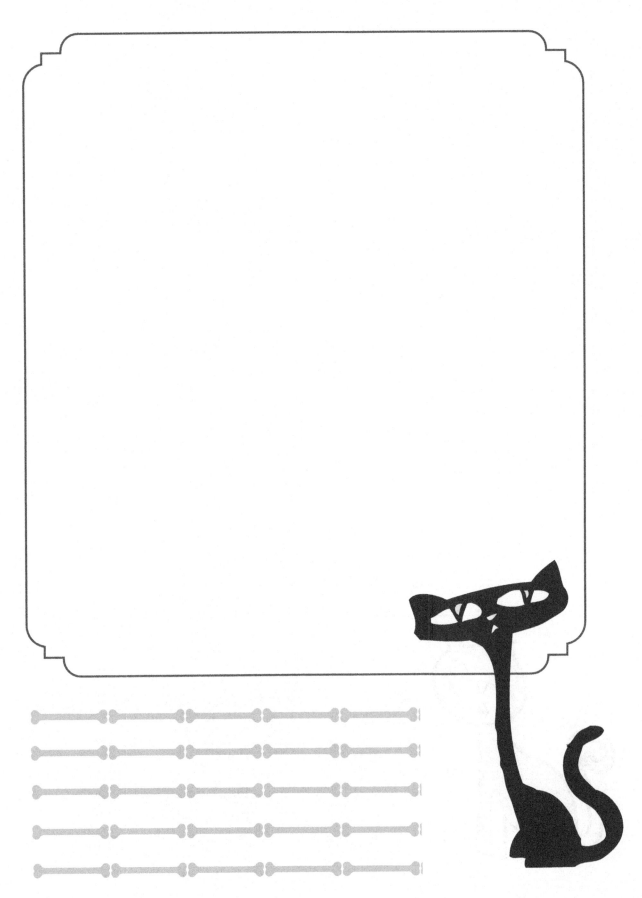

My bony kitty cat

My pearl kitty cat

My kangaroo kitty cat

My crystal kitty cat

My purple eyed kitty cat

My hamburger kitty cat

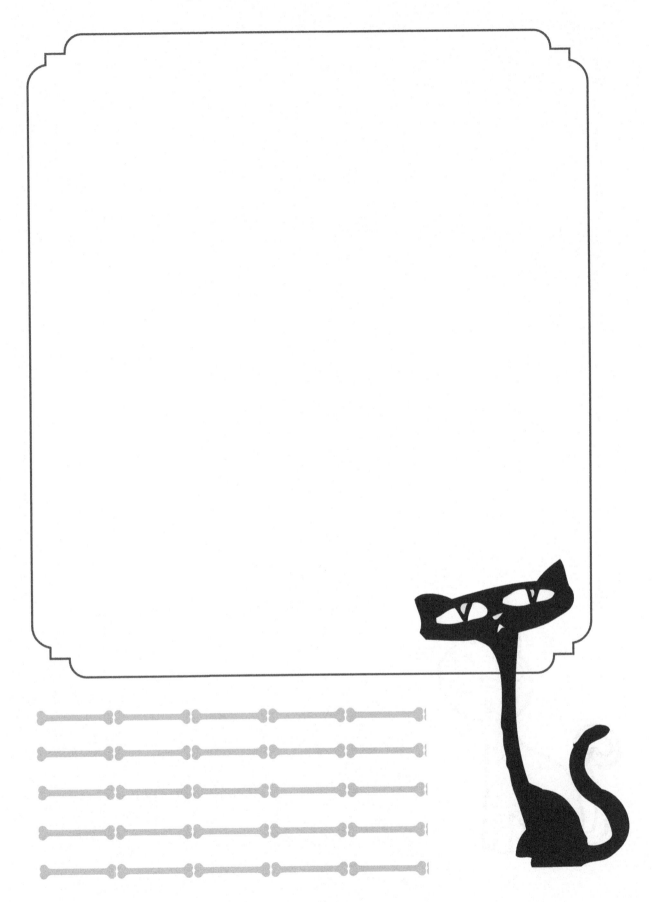

My sailor kitty cat

My wooden kitty cat

My curly kitty cat

My sister kitty cat

My chocolate chip kitty cat

My rose kitty cat

My chef kitty cat

My spaghetti kitty cat

My strange kitty cat

My box kitty cat

My basketball kitty cat

My rock n roll kitty cat

My squatty kitty cat

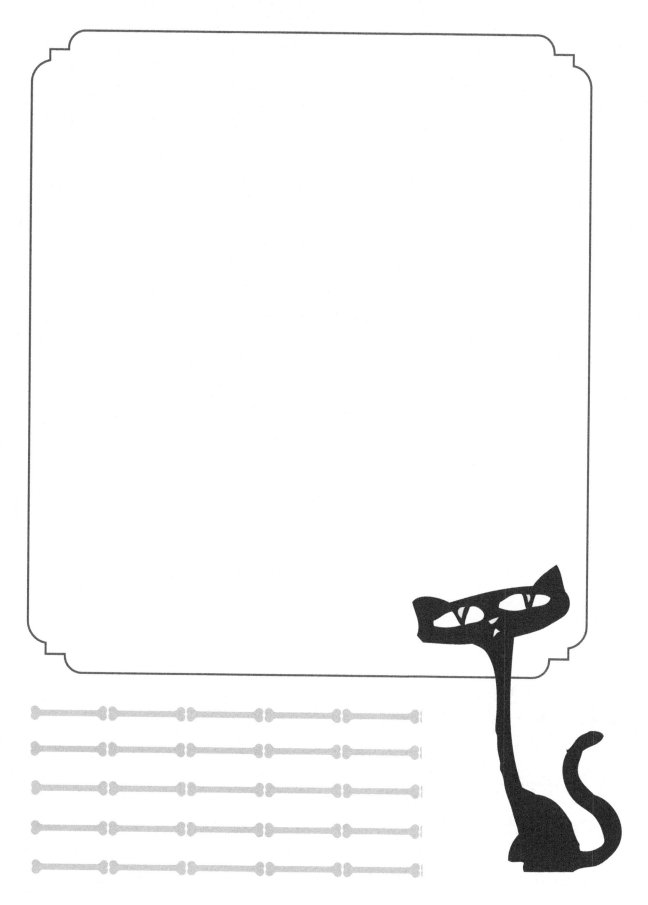

My lady kitty cat

My wild kitty cat

My goldfish kitty cat

My wrinkly kitty cat

My rocket kitty cat

My mermaid kitty cat

My smelly kitty cat

My orange striped kitty cat

My bandit kitty cat

My sleeping kitty cat

My stretching kitty cat

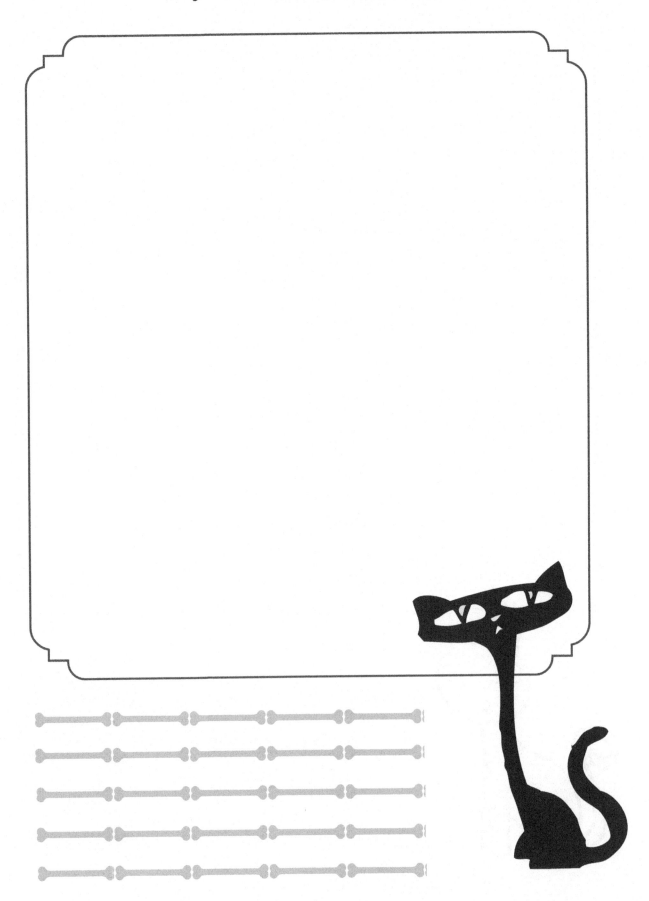

My bronze kitty cat

My salmon kitty cat

My pillow kitty cat

My piano kitty cat

My muddy kitty cat

My turquoise spotted kitty cat

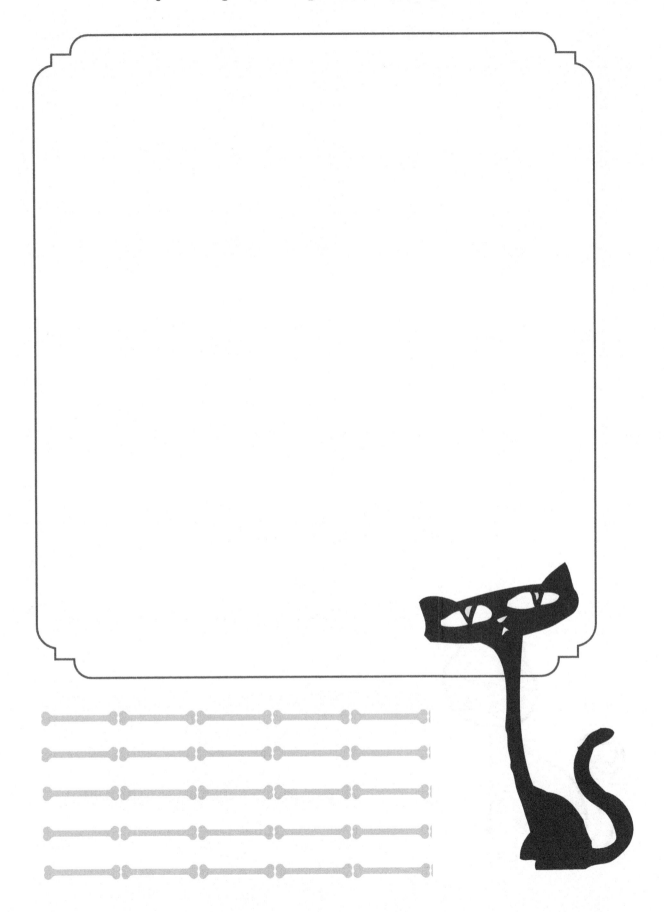

My tip toed kitty cat

My long haired kitty cat

My rainbow kitty cat

My boot wearing kitty cat

My bunny earred kitty cat

My ugly kitty cat

My walrus kitty cat

My crowned kitty cat

My no tailed kitty cat

My patchwork kitty cat

My artistic kitty cat

My snowflake kitty cat

My peanut butter kitty cat

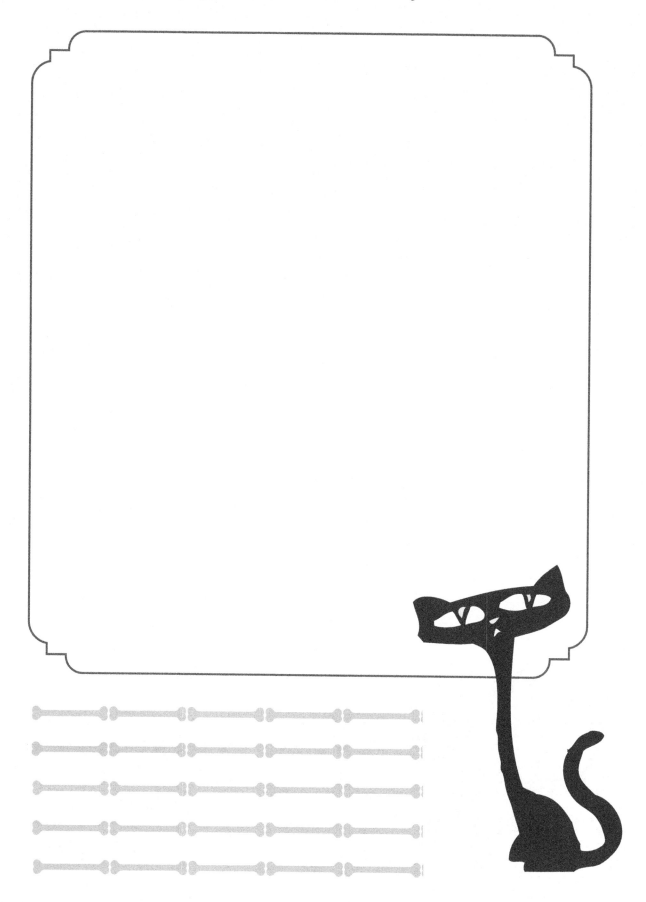

My high heeled kitty cat

My cactus kitty cat

My peaceful kitty cat

My tattooed kitty cat

My vampire kitty cat

My amethyst kitty cat

My yellow bellied kitty cat

My sweet kitty cat

My magenta kitty cat

My turtle kitty cat

My latte kitty cat

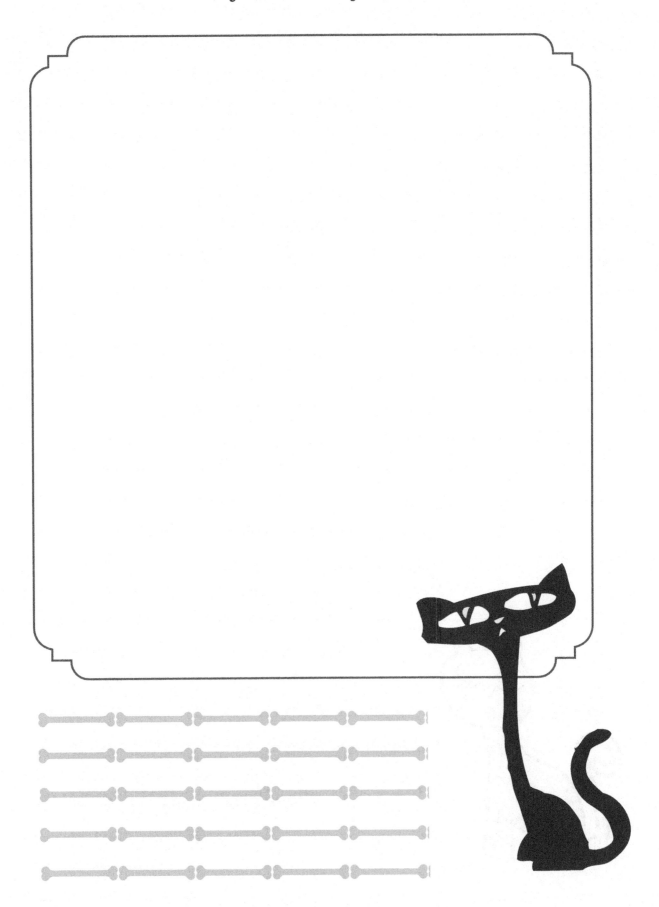

My red eyed kitty cat

My hot dog kitty cat

My pirate kitty cat

My ribbony kitty cat

My wheel-chaired kitty cat

My granny kitty cat

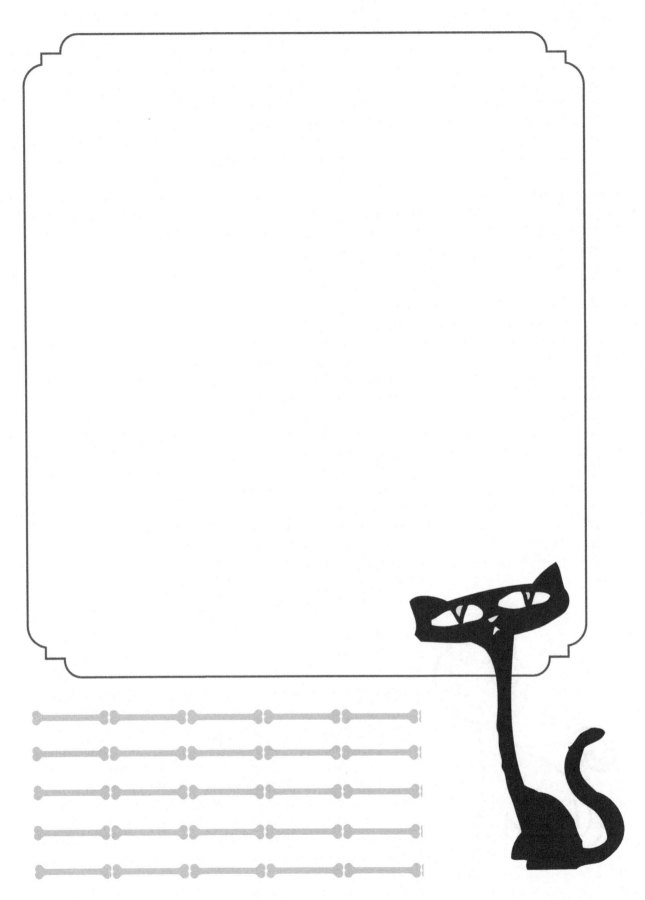

My swirled kitty cat

My wooden kitty cat

My cloud kitty cat

My cheering kitty cat

My lunar kitty cat

My penguin kitty cat

My pizza kitty cat

My young kitty cat

My tomato kitty cat

My movie star kitty cat

My crabby kitty cat

My cocoa kitty cat

My wonderful kitty cat

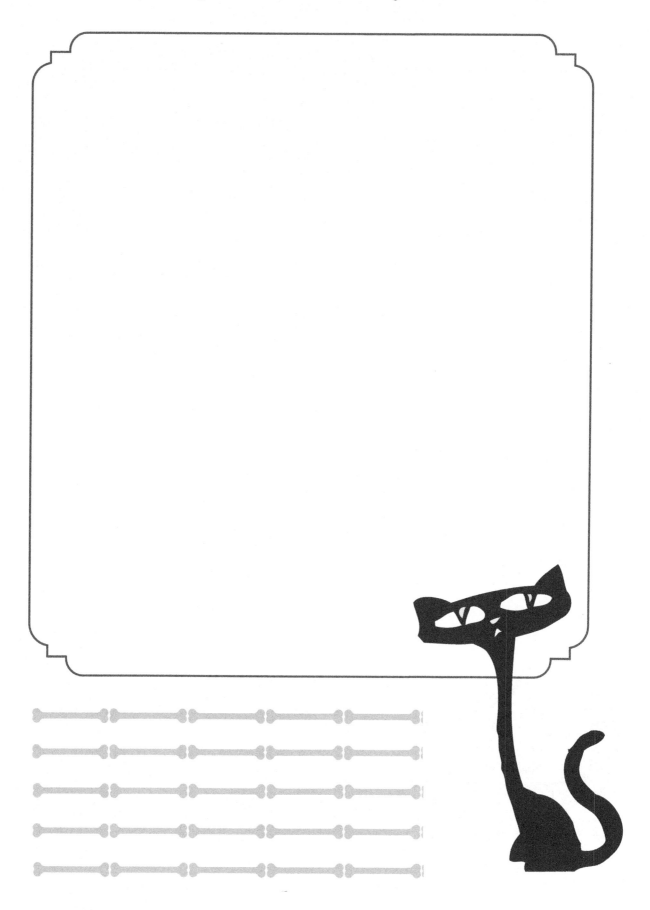

My bell wearing kitty cat

My scaly kitty cat

My UFO kitty cat

My fat kitty cat

My lucky kitty cat

My purple striped kitty cat

My puppet kitty cat

My red furred kitty cat

My dandelion kitty cat

My velvet kitty cat

My fluttering kitty cat

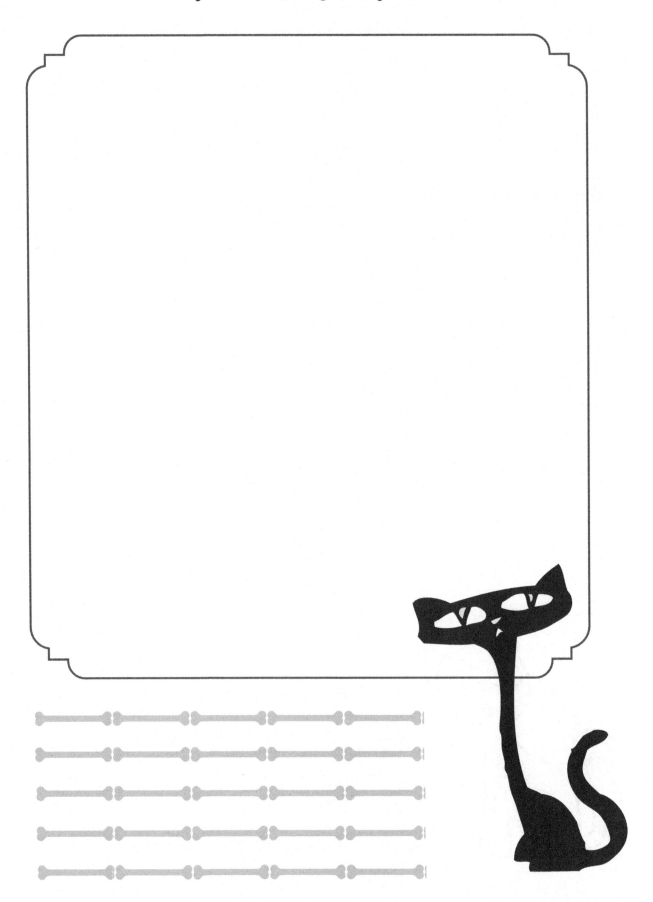

My horned kitty cat

My black striped kitty cat

My helicopter kitty cat

My money kitty cat

My brownie kitty cat

My blonde kitty cat

My pebbled kitty cat

My wooden kitty cat

My coral kitty cat

My pilgrim kitty cat

My hissing kitty cat

My funny kitty cat

My bubble kitty cat

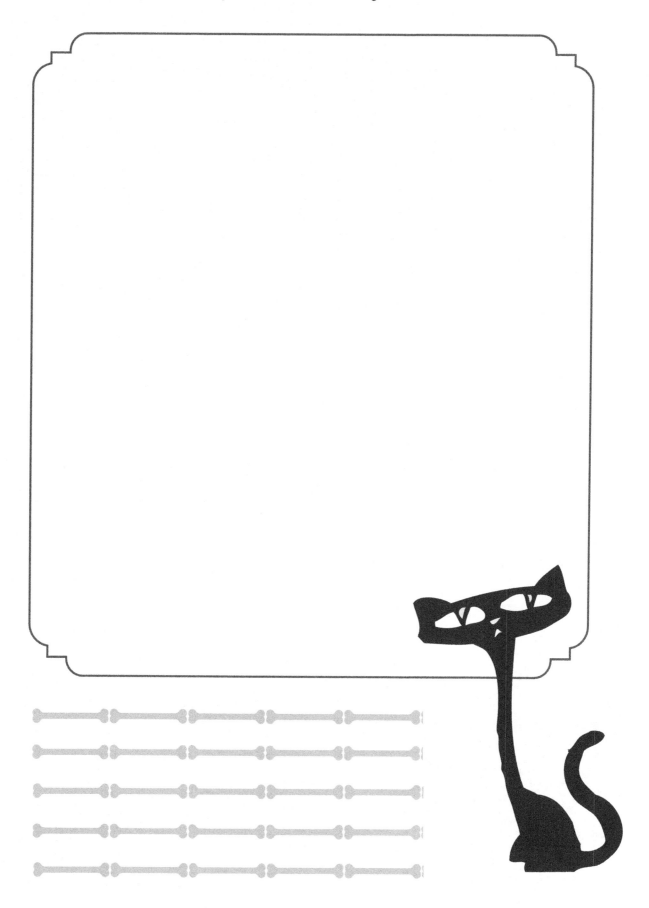

My alligator kitty cat

My jolly kitty cat

Made in the USA
Columbia, SC
27 April 2022